Court of Appeals of the District of Columbia

Court of Appeals, District of Columbia

The Washington Asphalt Block and Tile Company, A Corporation Appellant

No. 919

Court of Appeals of the District of Columbia

Court of Appeals, District of Columbia
The Washington Asphalt Block and Tile Company, A Corporation Appellant No. 919

ISBN/EAN: 9783744702195

Printed in Europe, USA, Canada, Australia, Japan

Cover: Foto ©Suzi / pixelio.de

More available books at **www.hansebooks.com**

TRANSCRIPT OF RECORD.

Court of Appeals, District of Columbia

OCTOBER TERM, 1899.

No. 919.

THE WASHINGTON ASPHALT BLOCK AND TILE
COMPANY, A CORPORATION, APPELLANT,

vs.

FRANKLIN H. MACKEY, ADMINISTRATOR OF THE
ESTATE OF CHARLES A. MARTIN.

APPEAL FROM THE SUPREME COURT OF THE DISTRICT OF COLUMBIA.

FILED JULY 7, 1899.

COURT OF APPEALS OF THE DISTRICT OF COLUMBIA.

OCTOBER TERM, 1899.

No. 919.

THE WASHINGTON ASPHALT BLOCK AND TILE
COMPANY, A CORPORATION, APPELLANT,

vs.

FRANKLIN H. MACKEY, ADMINISTRATOR OF THE
ESTATE OF CHARLES A. MARTIN.

APPEAL FROM THE SUPREME COURT OF THE DISTRICT OF COLUMBIA.

INDEX.

JUDD & DETWEILER, PRINTERS, WASHINGTON, D. C., JULY 20, 1899.

In the Court of Appeals of the District of Columbia

THE WASHINGTON ASPHALT BLOCK AND TILE COM-
pany, a Corporation, Appellant,
vs.
FRANKLIN H. MACKEY, Adm'r, &c.

} No. 919.

---

a   Supreme Court of the District of Columbia.

FRANKLIN H. MACKEY, Adm'r, &c.,
vs.
THE WASHINGTON ASPHALT BLOCK AND
Tile Company, a Corporation.

} No. 41905.   At Law.

UNITED STATES OF AMERICA, } *ss:*
   District of Columbia,

Be it remembered that in the supreme court of the District of
Columbia, at the city of Washington, in said District, at the times
hereinafter mentioned, the following papers were filed and proceed-
ings had in the above-entitled cause, to wit:

1   *Declaration.*

Filed March 1, 1898.

In the Supreme Court of the District of Columbia.

FRANKLIN H. MACKEY, Administrator of the
Estate of Charles A. Martin, Deceased, Plain-
tiff,
vs.
THE WASHINGTON ASPHALT BLOCK AND TILE
Company, a Corporation, Defendant.

} Law.   No. 41905.

The plaintiff, administrator of the estate of Charles A. Martin,
deceased, sues the defendant, The Washington Asphalt Block and
Tile Company, a corporation doing business in the District of Columbia, for that, to wit, on the 24th day of July, A. D. 1897, in the
District of Columbia, the said Martin being then and there in the
employ of the defendant, the defendant then and there was unloading at its wharf a certain boat or scow loaded with broken stone,
the process of unloading being substantially as follows: A number
of large iron buckets or receptacles for broken stone were filled,
each in turn, with said broken stone upon said boat or scow and
were then, each in turn, lifted by a steam hoisting machine from

1—919A

2 THE WASHINGTON ASPHALT BLOCK AND TILE CO.,

said boat or scow to the wharf. Attached to each of said buckets was a large iron handle, working upon pivots affixed to the side of said buckets, the said handle being intended to remain in an upright position while said buckets are being loaded and to be kept in such position by a mechanical contrivance for that purpose affixed to said handle. On the day and date aforesaid, at

2   the place aforesaid, the said Martin, who was then and there in the service and employ of the defendant, was engaged, with other employees of the defendant, in placing or throwing said stone into one of said buckets, and while standing, without any negligence, upon said boat or scow near the said bucket the upright handle thereof, by reason of the bad order and worn condition of said contrivance for holding it in its upright position, suddenly fell from its said position, and in falling struck said Martin with great force, throwing him overboard, whereby his death almost immediately resulted from drowning; and the plaintiff says that the bad order and worn condition of said contrivance for holding said handle in position existed by reason of the negligence of the defendant, whose duty it was to keep the same in such proper order and condition as would prevent the accidental falling of said handle; and the plaintiff further says that the said injury to said Martin which resulted in his death, as aforesaid, was such that if death had not resulted therefrom would have entitled him to recover damages of the defendant. The said Martin left surviving him his widow and one child, an infant son of about one year of age, who have suffered great pecuniary loss by reason of his death. Wherefore the plaintiff, by reason of the statute in that behalf enacted, has become entitled to recover damages of the defendant for the benefit of said widow and son, and he claims, therefore, from the defendant the sum of ten thousand dollars, to be assessed as by the statute is enacted, together with costs.

2.

The plaintiff, administrator, as aforesaid, further sues the defendant, The Washington Asphalt Block and Tile Company, a

3   corporation doing business in the District of Columbia, for that, to wit, on the 24th day of July, A. D. 1897, in the District of Columbia, the said Martin being then and there in the employ of the defendant, the defendant then and there was unloading at its wharf a certain boat or scow loaded with broken stone, the process of unloading being substantially as follows : A number of large iron buckets or receptacles for broken stone were filled, each in turn, with said broken stone upon said boat or scow and were then, each in turn, lifted by a steam hoisting machine from said boat or scow to the wharf. Attached to each of said buckets was a large iron handle, working upon pivots affixed to the side of said buckets, the said handle being intended to remain in an upright position while said buckets are being loaded and to be kept in such position by a mechanical contrivance for that purpose affixed to said handle. On the day and date aforesaid, at the place aforesaid, the said Martin, who was then and there in the service

and employ of the defendant, was engaged, with other employees of the defendant, in placing or throwing said stone into one of said buckets, and while standing, without any negligence, upon said boat or scow near the said bucket the upright handle thereof, by reason of the said contrivance for holding said handle in its upright position being insufficient in its construction for the purposes for which said bucket was used, to wit, unloading stone, as aforesaid, said insufficiency being then and there unknown to said Martin (the service or labor in which said Martin was engaged not being in itself dangerous), suddenly fell from its upright position, and in falling struck said Martin with great force, knocking him overboard, whereby his death almost immediately resulted from drowning; and the plaintiff says that other and better con-
4   trivances could have been adopted and used by the defendant for the purpose aforesaid, and the defendant negligently failed to adopt and use said other and better contrivances, which negligent failure, as aforesaid, caused the injury and death of said Martin; and the plaintiff further says that the said injury to said Martin which resulted in his death, as aforesaid, was such that if death had not resulted therefrom would have entitled him to recover damages of the defendant. The said Martin left surviving him his widow and one child, an infant son of about one year of age, who have suffered great pecuniary loss by reason of his death.

Wherefore plaintiff, by reason of the statute in that behalf enacted, has become entitled to recover damages of the defendant for the benefit of said widow and son, and he claims, therefore, from the defendant the sum of ten thousand dollars, to be assessed as by the statute is enacted, together with costs.

FRANKLIN H. MACKEY,
Attorney for Plaintiff.

The defendant is to plead hereto on or before the twentieth day, exclusive of Sundays and legal holidays, occurring after the day of service hereof; otherwise judgment.

FRANKLIN H. MACKEY,
Attorney for Plaintiff.

5   *Pleas.*

Filed March 25, 1898.

In the Supreme Court of the District of Columbia.

FRANKLIN H. MACKEY, Administrator of the Estate of Charles A. Martin, Deceased, Plaintiff,

vs.

THE WASHINGTON ASPHALT BLOCK AND Tile Company, a Corporation, Defendant.

At Law.   No. 41905.

Comes now here the defendant, and for plea to both of the counts of the plaintiff's declaration says—
That it is not guilty as alleged.

BIRNEY & WOODARD,
Attorneys for Defendant.

Additional Plea, &c.

Filed May 29, 1899.

In the Supreme Court of the District of Columbia.

FRANKLIN H. MACKEY, Adm'r of the Estate of Charles
 A. Martin, Dec.,
 vs.   } No. 41905.
WASHINGTON ASPHALT BLOCK & TILE COMPANY, Defendant.

6   Now comes the defendant, and for further plea, by leave of the
court *filed*, says that the plaintiff is not and never was administrator of the estate of the said Charles A. Martin in
manner and form as alleged in the declaration.

BIRNEY & WOODARD,
Attorneys for Defendant.

DISTRICT OF COLUMBIA, *ss :*

I, Arthur A. Birney, on oath say that I am of counsel for the
defendant in the above-entitled cause; that it affirmatively appears
by the records of the orphans' court of the supreme court of the
District of Columbia, by which court the letters of administration
alleged in the declaration were granted Franklin H. Mackey, as
alleged in his declaration in this cause, that said intestate, Charles
A. Martin, left no estate, either real or personal, in the District of
Columbia at his death; wherefore I say that said court was without
jurisdiction to grant letters of administration, and the alleged letters
of administration issued to the said Mackey were and are void, and
he, the said Mackey, is not and never was administrator of said
Charles A. Martin, deceased.

ARTHUR A. BIRNEY.

Sworn to before me this 29th day of May, 1899.

J. R. YOUNG, *Clerk,*
By ALF. G. BUHRMAN, *Ass't Cl'k.*

7   *Joinder of Issue.*

Filed March 28, 1898.

In the Supreme Court of the District of Columbia.

FRANKLIN H. MACKEY, Adm'r, &c.,
 vs.   } Law. No. 41905.
THE WASHINGTON ASPHALT BLOCK & TILE Co.

The plaintiff joins issue on the defendant's plea.

FRANKLIN H. MACKEY, *P. P.*

Memorandum.

June 1, 1899.—Verdict for plaintiff for $5,000.00.

Supreme Court of the District of Columbia.

WEDNESDAY, *June* 21, 1899.

Session resumed pursuant to adjournment, Chief Justice Bingham presiding.

> FRANKLIN H. MACKEY, Administrator of the
> Estate of Charles A. Martin, Dec'd, Pl't'ff,
>   *vs.*   } At Law. No. 41905.
> THE WASHINGTON ASPHALT BLOCK AND TILE
> Company, a Corporation, Defendant.

This cause coming on to be heard upon the defendant's motion for a new trial, and the same having been heard, it is considered that said motion be, and hereby is, overruled and judgment on verdict ordered. Therefore it is considered that the plaintiff recover against the defendant five thousand dollars ($5,000.00) damages, as aforesaid assessed, together with his costs of suit, to be taxed by the clerk, and have execution thereof.

Order for Appeal, &c.

Filed June 22, 1899.

In the Supreme Court of the District of Columbia.

> FRANKLIN H. MACKEY, Adm'r of the Estate
> of Chas. A. Martin,
>   *vs.*   } No. 41905. At Law.
> THE WASHINGTON ASPHALT BLOCK & TILE
> Co.

Now comes the defendant and appeals from the judgment on the verdict in this cause to the Court of Appeals of the District of Columbia.

BIRNEY & WOODARD,
Attorneys for Defendant.

June 22, 1899.

The clerk will pleass issue citation to appellee.

BIRNEY & WOODARD,
Attorneys for Defendant.

In the Supreme Court of the District of Columbia.

> FRANKLIN H. MACKEY, Administrator of the
> Estate of Charles A. Martin,
>   *vs.*   } At Law. No. 41905.
> THE WASHINGTON ASPHALT BLOCK AND
> Tile Company, a Corporation.

The President of the United States to Franklin H. Mackey, administrator of the estate of Charles A. Martin, Greeting:

You are hereby cited and admonished to be and appear at a Court of Appeals of the District of Columbia, upon the docketing the cause therein under and as directed by the rules of said court, pursuant to an appeal filed in the supreme court of the District of Columbia on the 22d day of June, 1899, wherein The Washington Asphalt Block and Tile Company, a corporation, is appellant and you are appellee, to show cause, if any there be, why the judgment rendered against the said appellant should not be corrected and why speedy justice should not be done to the parties in that behalf.

Witness the Honorable Edward F. Bingham, chief justice of the supreme court of the District of Columbia, this 22 day of June, in the year of our Lord one thousand eight hundred and ninety-nine.

Seal Supreme Court of the District of Columbia.

JOHN R. YOUNG, *Clerk.*

Service of the above citation accepted this 22d day of June, A. D. 1899.

FRANKLIN H. MACKEY,
Attorney for Appellee.

10   *Memorandum.*

June 28, 1899.—Appeal bond filed.

Supreme Court of the District of Columbia.

WEDNESDAY, *May* 28, 1899.

Session resumed pursuant to adjournment, Chief Justice Bingham presiding.

*   *   *   *   *   *   *

FRANKLIN H. MACKEY, Adm'r, Plaintiff, }
vs. } At Law.   No. 41905.
WASHINGTON ASPHALT BLOCK & TILE Co., }
Defendant. }

Now again comes here the defendant and tenders to the court here its bill of exceptions taken during the trial hereof and prays that the same may be duly signed, sealed, and made part of the record, now for then, which is done accordingly.

11   *Bill of Exceptions.*

Filed June 28, 1899.

In the Supreme Court of the District of Columbia.

FRANKLIN H. MACKEY, Administrator of }
the Estate of Charles A. Martin, Deceased, }
vs. } At Law.   No. 41905.
WASHINGTON ASPHALT BLOCK AND TILE }
Company. }

Be it remembered that on the trial of this cause the plaintiff, to maintain the issues on his part joined, offered to read in evidence a certain record of the probate court of the supreme court of the District of Columbia, being a petition of Franklin H. Mackey, an order passed thereon by said court, and letters of administration issued to the plaintiff, Franklin H. Mackey; to the reading of which in evidence the defendant, by its attorney, then and there objected on the ground that it appears from said record that the said probate court was without jurisdiction to grant letters of administration in the premises, and that said letters of administration are void; but the justice presiding overruled said objection; to which ruling the defendant, by its attorney, then and there duly excepted, and said exception was noted on the minutes of the said justice, and the said petition and order and the letters of administration granted thereon and dated February 11, 1898, were read in evidence to the jury as follows:

12   In the Supreme Court of the District of Columbia, Holding a Special Term for Orphans' Court Business.

In re Estate of CHARLES A. MARTIN, Deceased.

The petition of Franklin H. Mackey respectfully shows that he is a citizen of the United States and a resident of the District of Columbia.

That Charles A. Martin, late a resident of the District of Columbia and domiciled therein at the time of his death, departed this life on the 24th day of July, A. D. 1897, intestate and leaving surviving him his widow, Alice M. Martin, and an infant son, Charles A. Martin, aged one year, as his only heirs-at-law. Both widow and son reside in the District of Columbia.

The deceased left no property, real or personal. His death was caused by the negligence, as petitioner is informed and believes, of the Washington Asphalt Block and Tile Company, a corporation doing business in the District of Columbia, and in whose employ the deceased was at the time of his death.

By reason of said negligence a right has accrued to said widow and child to bring an action, through an administrator, duly appointed, for the recovery of damages.

Your petitioner has been requested by said widow to apply for said letters, as will appear by the letter of request and affidavit hereto annexed.

Wherefore petitioner prays that he may be appointed such 13   administrator, and that letters may issue to him upon his qualifying in such manner as the court may require.

And your petitioner will ever pray, etc.

FRANKLIN H. MACKEY.

Franklin H. Mackey, being duly sworn, deposes and says that he has read the foregoing petition subscribed by him and knows the contents thereof; that the facts therein stated upon his personal knowledge are true, and those stated upon information and belief he believes to be true.

FRANKLIN H. MACKEY.

Subscribed and sworn to before me this 3d day of February, 1898.

M. J. GRIFFETH,
Notary Public.

CITY OF WASHINGTON, }
District of Columbia, } *ss :*

Alice M. Martin, being duly sworn, deposes and says that she is the widow of Charles A. Martin, deceased, who departed this life intestate on the 24th day of July, 1897, leaving no property, personal or real, of any value; that deceased'- death was caused, as affiant is informed and believes, by the negligent act of the Washington Asphalt Block and Tile Company, a corporation doing business in the District of Columbia; that affiant and her son, Charles A. Martin, aged eighteen months, are the only next of kin of deceased; affiant is desirous that an action be brought to re-
14   cover damages growing out of the death of her said husband, and prays the court having jurisdiction in the premises to appoint Franklin H. Mackey, Esq., administrator for this purpose.

ALICE M. MARTIN.

Subscribed and sworn to before me this 3d day of February, A. D. 1898.

M. J. GRIFFETH,
Notary Public.

15   In the Supreme Court of the District of Columbia, Holding an Orphans' Court.

In re Estate of CHARLES A. MARTIN, Deceased.   No. 8193.

On reading the petition for letters of administration filed herein and on consideration thereof, it is this 11th day of February, A. D. 1898, adjudged, ordered, and decreed that Franklin H. Mackey, Esq., be, and he is hereby, appointed administrator of the estate of Charles A. Martin, deceased, upon his qualifying and giving bond in the penalty of three hundred dollars, conditioned for the faithful performance of his trust.

A. B. HAGNER,
Associate Justice.

In the Supreme Court of the District of Columbia, Holding a Special Term for Orphans' Court Business.

DISTRICT OF COLUMBIA, *To wit :*

The United States of America to all persons to whom these presents shall come, Greeting :

Know ye that whereas Charles A. Martin, late of the District of Columbia, has died intestate, as it is said, on the 24th day of July, A. D. 1897, leaving certain goods, chattels, and personal estate to be administered :

Now, know ye that administration of all the goods, chattels, and credits of the deceased is hereby granted and committed unto Franklin H. Mackey, of the District of Columbia.

Witness A. B. Hagner, justice holding the special term of the said supreme court for orphans' court business, this eleventh day of February, in the year of our Lord one thousand eight hundred and ninety-eight, and of the Independence of the United States the one hundred and twenty-second.

Test:
J. NOTA McGILL,
Register of Wills for the District of Columbia.

16   Thereupon the plaintiff read in evidence the deposition of one BURTON DE VAUGHN, taken *de bene esse*, the same being in substance as follows:

That on the 24th day of July, 1897, witness was a laborer in the employ of the defendant, Washington Asphalt Block and Tile Company, and in company with the decedent was engaged in the work of unloading a scow loaded with stone, such scow being moored at the wharf of the defendant, at the foot of South Capitol street, Washington, D. C., there being a space of about 2½ feet between the scow and the wharf. In unloading the scow a large iron tub was used. This tub, after being filled by the men on the boat with broken stones, was hoisted by means of a crane to a tower above, where a roller was forced against the trigger of the handle of the tub, whereby the tub was dumped, said derrick or crane being operated by steam. The tub is a little heavier on one side than on the other, so that when the trigger or latch was knocked back the tub turned almost upside down. Said Charles A. Martin and the witness were loading one tub, and Henry T. Martin, a brother of the deceased, and a colored man were loading a similar tub on the other side of the scow. Said Charles A. Martin stood right on the side of the scow, his heels touching the side of the scow as it went up and down. He was standing about a foot and a half from the tub, and witness was on the opposite side of the tub. Both were loading the tub with stones, which they picked up and threw into it. The stones were of various sizes, some being as large as a man's head and some
17   considerably larger; and the witness, being asked to state how the said Charles A. Martin happened to fall overboard, answered: " Well, as he and I was loading the tub, he was reaching after a stone or had a stone going up to put into the tub. I threw a stone into the tub, and it hit another stone, which bounded and hit the trigger of the tub and knocked the handle back against him and knocked him overboard;" and witness, being asked to describe the handle of the tub, testified that such handle is made of iron about an inch and a half square, with a big eye on the top of it, in which the lift-rope or cable may be fastened; that such handle would weight at least one hundred pounds and was fastened on the sides like the handle of any ordinary bucket, but was held upright by a latch or trigger of iron, which works on a pivot in the handle directly under the eye aforesaid, from which it extends at right angles to the handle to and beyond

the rim of the bucket on one side; that in said latch is a notch or cut which, when the handle of the bucket is upright and supported by said latch, fits over and upon a small steel roller fastened to the side of said bucket, to which roller the trigger is not fastened except by pressure of its own weight; that said trigger at its upper end extends a few inches beyond said handle, and when the engine has lifted the tub into the tower aforesaid this part of the trigger comes in contact with the roller and is by it pressed down so as to lift the other end of the trigger up and off the roller aforesaid; whereupon the tub turns over. Said witness further testified that the stone thrown in by him struck another piece of stone and then struck this latch and knocked it up and off the roller
18   aforesaid, and that the handle thereupon fell and said Martin fell overboard; that he struggled in the water about a second and then sank and was drowned; that said Martin was 23 or 24 years of age, a well and strong man; earned a dollar and a half a day; had been married not quite two years, and left a widow and infant child surviving him; and said witness being asked the following question: "This latch which supports this handle, I wish you to state in what condition it was in regard to being new or worn or out of order or in order; state what you know about that," answered as follows: "Well, it was not in the best of order; it had been worn some; if it had been tighter, it would not have been easy to knock off;" and being asked how long he had worked with the said tubs answered, "I worked there three or four days."

And upon cross-examination said witness testified that he had worked there about two or three days and had never worked at that business before; that the bucket at the time he threw in the stone was about three-fourths full; that the stone weighed about forty pounds, and was a flat, heavy, large stone; that he threw it in and it hit the other stone and glanced around and knocked the latch loose, striking it a pretty hard blow; that the stone thrown was about eleven inches wide on the top and three or four inches on one side and maybe a little thicker on the other; that he did not know how long the bucket had been in use; and being asked whether it was a new bucket or an old bucket answered, "It did not look to be a new bucket; it had been worn," and that that was all he
19   knew of it; that he did not know on what part of his person the handle struck Martin, but when the handle fell Martin was stooping over, and that he, the witness, was about two feet from the bucket when he threw in the stone.

And plaintiff offered further evidence by one HENRY T. MARTIN, brother of said decedent, tending to show that the said Charles A. Martin at the time of his death had been working for the defendant company about one month; that the scow which was being unloaded was about 12 feet wide and the stone was upon its deck; that the bucket in question was substantially as described by the witness De Vaughn and was like an iron model which was produced in evidence, except that it had not upon it an iron latch attached to the said model so produced; that the bucket in question was about 2½ feet one way and about three feet the other way, and the

handle thereof would weigh about 100 pounds. Said Charles A.
Martin earned at the business at which he was engaged about $1.50
a day.

Said plaintiff further called as a witness one Louis Beyer, who
testified in substance that he had pursued in the city of Washington his business as machinist for many years and made the model
of bucket which was produced in court, as aforesaid, and which
was drawn on a scale of ¼ of an inch to an inch; that he examined
the original bucket in the possession of the defendant before mak-
ing the model and made measurements thereof, and that the bucket
offered in evidence is like the original, excepting only that on the
handle of the model and at one side of the trigger before described
the witness had attached a latch which when dropped into the
space between the trigger and the handle would so lock the
20   trigger as that it could not be easily knocked up and off the
roller at its lower end; and thereupon witness was asked
by counsel for plaintiff the following question : " Mr. Beyer, state
whether or not such a contrivance as this or a pin here or some
other contrivance to prevent this handle from falling over, some
simple contrivance of that sort, would suggest itself to any ordinary
mechanic whose attention had been called to the matter." To
which question counsel for the defendant then and there objected
on the ground that such inquiry was incompetent and immaterial,
but the justice presiding overruled said objection ; to which ruling
counsel for the defendant then and there duly excepted ; and the
witness thereupon answered the question, " Yes ; to any one ; any
common laborer would understand it."

The witness was further asked the following question : " What
would be the effect, Mr. Beyer, of the continued use of this latch
up and down on this catch (counsel referring to the trigger and
catch on the model of the bucket)?" To which the witness answered, " This (indicating the notch or cut on the trigger) would
wear out ; this friction roller would be smaller and then it would
be easy ; if you were to hit it, it would drop out." Witness was
thereupon asked the following question : " Could the falling of the
handle have been prevented in any easy or simple way?" To
which question counsel for the defendant then and there objected
on the ground that the same was incompetent and immaterial, but
the justice presiding overruled said objection ; to which overruling
counsel for the defendant then and there duly excepted.
21   Whereupon witness answered, " Why, yes," (inserting the
latch by him attached to the handle of the bucket); " now
it is prevented here. It could be prevented down here" (indicating
the side of the bucket near the lower part of the handle) " by a pin
or something, but this is the easiest way, to drop this down " (indicating the latch). " If you put a stone or something in, that
would prevent its falling or dropping." " Of course, where the
friction roller wears away it drops out quick." And on cross-
examination said witness testified that he had worked with buckets
like the bucket in question, but had never seen one upon which

there was a catch like that which he had attached to the bucket model then in court, and had never seen one with a pin in the side such as he had described as being sufficient to hold the handle, but the buckets he had seen in use, and like that which had been described in evidence, in use by said defendant at the time of the death of said Martin, were without such a catch or pin and made just as that bucket was made; that buckets of that type have been in use a number of years to his knowledge, but he did not know how many years or when they were invented, but it must have been a good many years that they have been in use.

And here the plaintiff rested, this being the substance of all the evidence offered by the plaintiff in chief.

And thereupon counsel for the defendant moved the court to instruct the jury to return a verdict for the defendant, on the ground that the plaintiff had failed to make out such a case as entitled him to have the cause submitted to the jury, but the justice presiding overruled said objection; to which ruling counsel for the defendant then and there duly excepted.

22   And thereupon the defendant, to maintain the issues on its part joined, called as a witness one P. J. HEFFRON, foreman of workmen for the defendant, who testified in substance that he had been employed by the defendant for about five years; that said defendant used four buckets of the kind described in evidence; that similar buckets are in use in the city of Washington by the Cranford Asphalt Paving Company and by the Barber Asphalt Paving Company; that such buckets are made by the Hunt Manufacturing Company of New York, which company puts up plants of this description all over the world, as the witness understood, and that such company does an extensive business in such manufactures; that ever since the death of Martin the buckets then in use have been used as before in the business of the company, and that the trigger of the bucket in question has not been changed in any way since the death of Martin and is yet in perfect condition; that the latches or triggers have worked perfectly at all times and there is no change in them from their first condition, but they are working just the same as when the defendant got them; and further testified that men using good judgment always put the handle down when loading the bucket, thereby enabling them to load it more easily; that when the tub is being loaded it should be set lengthwise the boat and the handle put down, but when Martin was injured the tub was set crosswise, so that the handle fell toward the edge of the boat; he further testified that in his opinion the catch or latch attached to the model by the witness Beyer would, if used upon buckets in actual use, be a source of danger to workmen, in that they would depend upon the latch, would not let the handle down as they should when loading, and would neglect to fasten it with the latch. Witness was thereupon interrogated by a juror as follows:

23   "If that catch were on there, it would prevent accidents, would it not?"

"A. It very likely would prevent an accident in loading the tub, but I never considered that there was any danger in loading the tub."

And further testified that he never had any reason to suppose that there was any danger to the men while loading the tub; that the rope which lifts the tub is detached from the tub while the same is being loaded and used in hoisting other tubs, and that he had never given the men instructions in what way to load the tub nor whether the handle should be put up or down; but the men had been in the habit of loading the tubs with the handle down and with the bucket or tub in position lengthwise of the scow, and that the scow was about 48 feet long by 15 or 17 feet wide, and was moored about 12 feet from the end of the wharf of the defendant, and that the water between the boat and the wharf might have been 18 feet deep.

And upon cross-examination the witness testified that the tub in question and the others like it in use by the defendant at the time of the trial had been used about five years; that they are used on an average about six months in each year and about four times a week in the six months, and that in a day's work each tub will carry up about 300 loads; that the handles and triggers on said tubs were put on about three years before the trial, the handles on the tubs when purchased having been afterward broken and taken
24   off; but said handles were not taken off because of wear, for
that they were not much worn. They had been worn more or less, but not so as to affect them, and that the handles and triggers now on said buckets are worn more or less, but are still in working order and just as safe as any new ones; and to the question "Then it has not been worn?" the witness answered, "It is worn less or more, but it is perfectly safe," and gave further evidence tending to show that *when* the bucket after being hoisted and emptied is again lowered to the deck of the boat, where it is received by the men who load it and is placed in position by them.

And here the defendant rested, this being all the evidence offered on its behalf.

Thereupon plaintiff offered evidence in rebuttal by the witness HENRY T. MARTIN tending to show that the witness had worked for the defendant in unloading scows of stone, and that he and the men who worked with him in loading always loaded the bucket with the handle upright, and that, so far as he knew, De Vaughn had loaded with the handle up; that nobody had instructed him how the tub was to be placed on the boat, but the foreman had told them to be particular; and here the plaintiff rested, this being in substance all the testimony taken in the case.
25   And thereupon the defendant, by its counsel, prayed the court to instruct the jury that under all the evidence in the cause the plaintiff was not entitled to recover, and that their verdict must be for the defendant, on the ground that the evidence in the cause was insufficient to warrant a verdict for the plaintiff; but the justice presiding refused to grant said prayer and to so

instruct the jury; to which refusal counsel for the defendant then and there duly excepted; and thereupon the defendant, by its counsel, prayed the court to instruct the jury that on the second count of the plaintiff's declaration he was not entitled to recover, and on that count the verdict must be for the defendant, on the grounds that no cause of action was shown by said second count, and that the evidence was insufficient to sustain a verdict for the plaintiff upon said count; but the justice presiding refused to give such instruction; to which refusal counsel for the defendant then and there duly excepted; and thereupon the justice presiding, at the request of counsel for plaintiff, gave to the jury three instructions, as follows:

"1. The jury are instructed that if they believe from the evidence that the latch to the bucket, as described in the evidence, was in a worn condition, and thereby rendered the bucket unsafe, and because of such worn condition the handle of the bucket fell and struck the deceased, causing his death, then the plaintiff is entitled to recover, provided the deceased did nothing to contribute to the accident by any negligence of his own."

"2. The jury are also instructed that if they believe that the bucket as used by the defendant was unsafe, but by a simple and easily applied contrivance patent to any mechanic of reasonable skillfulness it could have been rendered reasonably safe, so
26   that the accident described in the evidence would not have occurred, then the defendant is liable if the deceased was not himself guilty of any contributory negligence."

"3. If the jury find for the plaintiff, they should find such sum as will compensate the widow and child for such pecuniary loss as they have sustained by reason of the intestate's death, and in determining the amount to be awarded they should take into consideration the age of the deceased, his health, strength, capacity to earn money, and family, but their award must not exceed the sum of ten thousand dollars."

To the giving of each of which said first two instructions the counsel for the defendant then and there separately excepted; and thereupon and at the request of counsel for the defendant the justice presiding gave to the jury the following instructions:

"2a. To entitle the plaintiff to recover in this action the jury must be satisfied from a preponderance of the evidence that the bucket handle spoken of by the witnesses was defective and out of repair, and must further find that such want of repair or defective condition was known to the defendant through its officers or superintendent, or that it was so apparent or had continued so long that the defendant ought to have known of such want of repair or defect, and they must further find that such want of repair or defect in said bucket handle or its fastenings was the direct and proximate cause of the death of the plaintiff's intestate."

27   "3. The jury are instructed that it will not be enough to entitle the plaintiff to recover that they should find from the evidence that a defect existed in the bucket handle or the fastenings thereof, about which the witnesses have testified, but it must

also have been made affirmatively to appear, not as the result of conjecture, but as a legitimate inference from the evidence, both that the defect in question was the proximate cause of the death of the plaintiff's intestate, and that the defendant, The Washington Asphalt Block & Tile Company, through its officers or superintendent, knew or reasonably ought to have known of the existence of such defect and knew or reasonably should have known that such defect or want of repair would make the use of such bucket by its employés dangerous to them."

"4. The jury are instructed that there is no implied warranty on the part of a master that the tools furnished his servant or employé are sound and fit for the purpose intended, nor does a master become liable for an injury sustained by an employé from the use of a defective tool or instrument from the fact merely that such tool or implement or instrument was defective and might have been known to the master to be so defective, unless he also knew *or reasonably should have known* that the use of such tool in its defective condition would probably result in injury to the employé using it, and therefore if in this case the jury shall find from the evidence that the bucket handle in question and its appliances were unsound and out of repair, and that this want of repair was
28   known to the defendant, yet if they shall further find that
the defendant had no reason to know *or believe* that there was any probability of harm or injury to employés while loading or filling such bucket by reason of such defect or want of repair, the defendant should not be held liable, and the verdict should be in its favor."

"5. The jury are further instructed that if the bucket handle and its appliances were out of repair or otherwise defective, *as claimed in the declaration*, and this was known to the plaintiff's intestate, Martin, and that with such knowledge he continued to use such bucket and was injured thereby while so using it, the plaintiff cannot recover in this action."

"8. If the jury shall find from the evidence that at the time the plaintiff's intestate was struck by the handle or bucket in question he was standing on the extreme edge of the scow and in a position of danger, where a slight movement backwards would cause him to fall into the water, and further find that such position was a dangerous position, *such as would not be taken by a person of ordinary prudence* and not necessary to be taken by him in the discharge of his work *and was taken voluntarily by him*, and further find that when the bucket handle fell he would not have fallen overboard but for his being in such dangerous position, then they are instructed that they will be warranted in finding that the plaintiff's intestate contributed by his own negligence to his loss of life, and the plaintiff cannot recover."

29   And the defendant, by its counsel, further prayed the court
to instruct the jury as follows:

"The jury are instructed that the defendant was not bound to furnish for the use of plaintiff's intestate or its other employés any particular type of bucket or bucket handle or fastenings for such handle, nor was it bound in any way to provide any device or appliance for fastening such handle, and if the plaintiff's intestate lost his life by reason only that the bucket or its handle or other appliances were not provided with catches, locks, or other appliances to prevent the handle from falling, the plaintiff cannot recover in this action."

But the justice presiding refused to grant such instruction ; to which refusal counsel for the defendant then and there duly excepted.

And thereupon the justice presiding delivered to the jury an oral charge, in addition to the giving of the instructions so as aforesaid granted, and therein said : "It is the duty of the plaintiff in this case, before he can demand or ask of you a verdict, to convince you by the preponderance of the evidence, the entire evidence, that his charge against the defendant in one or the other or both of these counts is true. He must either convince you that the machinery in use and described in this count in the declaration was negligently permitted by the defendant to be used in and about its business, described in the declaration by the defendant, when it was in an unsafe and worn condition, or he must prove that the facts averred in the second count are true—that is, that it was
30   originally constructed imperfectly and not provided with such safe and proper appliances as a person of reasonable care and caution, exercising reasonable care and caution, would have provided.

If the plaintiff has convinced you by a preponderance of evidence that the facts stated in either one of these counts of the declaration are true, are proved, then the plaintiff is entitled to a verdict, unless you find that the plaintiff was himself guilty of negligence—that is, if he placed himself, for instance, in an insecure and improper position and was in an improper position at the time of the occurrence of this accident or that he knew of the defects in this machinery, whether they were such as came by use and wear or whether owing to their imperfect original construction and want of proper construction, of proper appliances, such as would be furnished by a person exercising ordinary care and prudence in the production and furnishing of such machines. If he knew that the machinery was faulty and defective and that danger might come from its use, from either cause or both, and continued in the service of the defendant until the accident occurred, the plaintiff is not in a condition to recover. The administrator of the deceased is not in a condition to demand damages of the defendant because of an accident which occurs under such circumstances ; " and said justice read to the jury the defendant's prayer marked " 2a" and added the words following : " Or, I must add to that, you must find that the machinery connected with this bucket, which has been testified to by the witnesses, was defective in its orig-
31   inal construction, and to an extent that in your judgment was required in order to make the use of the machinery safe and to be such machinery as would be furnished for such a purpose by a person in the exercise of ordinary care and prudence,"

and further said, "In regard to the question arising under the
second count of the declaration, something has been said by counsel in your presence and hearing with regard to the employment;
that the defendant should have furnished some particular fastenings or appliances to the handle and to the machinery connected
with the working of this bucket. The court will not instruct you
in regard to that, that it was essential that any special particular appliance should have been adopted in order to shield the defendant
from the consequences of this accident or to relieve *him* from the
action of the plaintiff at this time, and will only say to you, gentle-
men, that it is the duty of the defendant in furnishing this machinery to employés to furnish them with machinery that was so
constructed and planned as would make it reasonably safe to be
used and handled by the employés, and it should have been such
machinery and so regulated and planned as persons exercising ordinary care and prudence would plan and regulate in furnishing
such machinery for the use of their employés. About that the jury
has heard the testimony. They have seen the model produced here
and have heard the testimony and explanations of the witnesses.
They have heard the testimony in regard to how the accident occurred,
what position the parties were in at the time, and it is for you to
32   say from the evidence, taking the evidence and giving it care-
ful consideration, what relation, if any, the lack of the proper
construction of this machinery had to do with the occurrence of
this accident. If the evidence does not impress you by a preponderance of evidence as showing that there was any negligence
on the part of the defendants in furnishing this machinery, then,
for that reason, the defendant is not to be held liable; and should
you not find a like condition of things with reference to the charge
in the first count that the defendant permitted this machinery to
become worn by use and wear, so as to become imperfect and dangerous and to cause this accident to deceased—if you should not find
that by a preponderance of evidence and do not find the machinery
to be insufficient under the second count, you would for that reason
return a verdict for the defendant. On the contrary, if you find, as
I have stated to you in the first instance, that either there was a
defect in the machinery, as charged in the second count, under the
explanation and instructions which I have given you on that point,
or that there was a defective condition of the machinery by reason
of the use and wear of the same, which occasioned the accident to
the deceased, and that the deceased was not himself negligent—
guilty of a want of care with reference to his own safety—then you
will determine a verdict for the plaintiff for such damages with reference to the pecuniary injury which the next of kin have suffered
by his death as in your judgment would compensate them for such
    loss."
33   And thereupon and before the jury retired to consider
their verdict the defendant, by its counsel, duly excepted to
so much of the said charge as submitted to the jury the question
whether said bucket and its appliances were originally constructed
imperfectly and not provided with such safe and proper appliances
3—919A

as would be furnished by a person exercising ordinary care and
prudence in the production and furnishing of such machines, and
authorized the jury to find a verdict against the defendant if they
should find that the said bucket was defective in its original construction to an extent that, in the judgment of the jury, made such
bucket and its appliances unsafe to be used.

And all of the above exceptions so as above recited were sever-
ally and at the times of the taking of the same by the defendant
noted by the justice presiding on his minutes; and the defendant
now prays the court to sign this bill of exceptions, which is done,
now for then, this 28th day of June, 1899.

By the court:

E. F. BINGHAM, *C. J.* [SEAL.]

34   Supreme Court of the District of Columbia.

UNITED STATES OF AMERICA, }
   District of Columbia, } *ss :*

I, John R. Young, clerk of the supreme court of the District of Columbia, hereby certify the above and foregoing pages, numbered
from 1 to 33, inclusive, to be a true and correct transcript of the
record (as prescribed by rule 5 of the Court of Appeals of the District of Columbia) in cause No. 41905, at law, wherein Franklin H.
Mackey, adm'r, &c., is plaintiff and The Washington Asphalt Block
and Tile Company, a corporation, is defendant, as the same re-
mains upon the files and of record in said court.

In testimony whereof I hereunto subscribe
Seal Supreme Court my name and affix the seal of said court, at
  of the District of the city of Washington, in said District, this
  Columbia. 6th day of July, A. D. 1899.

JOHN R. YOUNG, *Clerk.*

Endorsed on cover : District of Columbia supreme court. No.
919. The Washington Asphalt Block and Tile Company, a corporation, appellant, *vs.* Franklin H. Mackey, adm'r, &c. Court of
Appeals, District of Columbia. Filed Jul- 7, 1899. Robert Willett,
clerk.